Ring-Tailed Lemurs

by Joelle Riley

Lerner Publications Company • Minneapolis

The images in this book are used with the permission of: © Nick Garbutt/Taxi/Getty Images, p. 4; © Laura Westlund/Independent Picture Service, p. 5; © Pete Oxford/Minden Pictures/ Getty Images, pp. 6, 8, 22, 30, 42; © age fotostock/SuperStock, pp. 7, 23; © Cyril Ruoso/JH Editorial/Minden Pictures/Getty Images, pp. 9, 15, 16, 19, 21, 24, 35, 43, 47; © Hermann Brehm/naturepl.com, p. 10; © Gerard Lacz/Peter Arnold, Inc., p. 11; © Kevin Schafer/Riser/ Getty Images, p. 12; © Biosphoto/Cyril Ruoso/Peter Arnold, Inc., p. 13; © Martin Harvey/Peter Arnold, Inc., p. 14; © Nick Garbutt/NHPA/Photoshot, pp. 17, 37, 38; © Martin Harvery/Gallo Images/Getty Images, p. 18; © Pete Oxford/naturepl.com, p. 20; © Stu Porter/Alamy, p. 25; © Roland Seitre/Peter Arnold, Inc., p. 26; © Kevin Schafer/NHPA/Photoshot, p. 27; © Holger Ehlers/Alamy, p. 28; © Eric Renard/RenardPhotos.com/Acclaim Images, p. 29; © Patricio Robles Gil/Sierra Madre/Minden Pictures/Getty Images, p. 31; © Doug Allen/The Image Bank/ Getty Images, p. 32; © Konrad Wothe/Minden Pictures/Getty Images, p. 33; © Frans Lanting/ CORBIS, p. 34; © Nick Garbutt/naturepl.com, pp. 36, 39; © Michael Fay/National Geographic/Getty Images, p. 40; © William F. Campbell/Time & Life Pictures/Getty Images, p. 41; © John Downer/Taxi/Getty Images, p. 46; © Martin Harvey/Digital Vision/Getty Images, p. 48.

Front Cover: © Pete Oxford/Minden Pictures/Getty Images.

Lerner Publications Company
A division of Lerner Publishing Group, Inc.
241 First Avenue North
Minneapolis, Minnesota 55401 U.S.A.

Website address: www.lernerbooks.com

Library of Congress Cataloging-in-Publication Data

Riley, Joelle.
    Ring-tailed lemurs / by Joelle Riley.
        p.   cm. — (Early bird nature books)
    Includes index.
    ISBN: 978–0–8225–9434–5 (lib. bdg. : alk. paper)
    1. Ring-tailed lemur—Juvenile literature. I. Title.
QL737.P95R55 2009
599.8'3—dc22   2008025632

Manufactured in the United States of America
1 2 3 4 5 6 – BP – 14 13 12 11 10 09

Contents

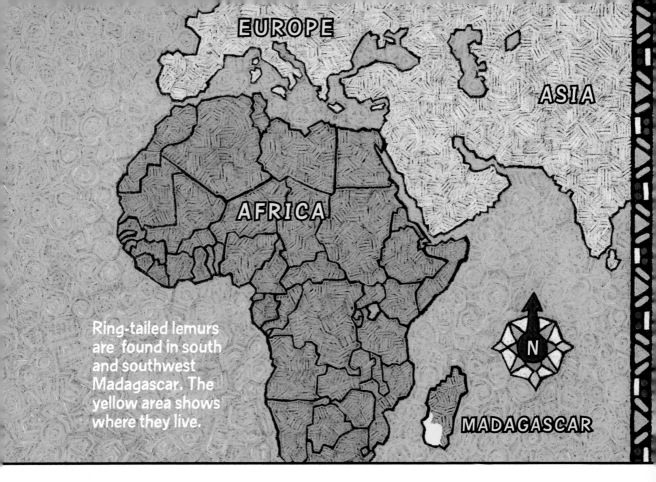

EUROPE

ASIA

AFRICA

Ring-tailed lemurs are found in south and southwest Madagascar. The yellow area shows where they live.

N

MADAGASCAR

Be a Word Detective

Can you find these words as you read about the ring-tailed lemur's life? Be a detective and try to figure out what they mean. You can turn to the glossary on page 46 for help.

dew	nursing	species
diurnal	predators	toothcomb
grooming	primates	troop
habitat	scent	
home range	social	

Chapter 1

These animals are ring-tailed lemurs. Where do ring-tailed lemurs live?

Lemurs with Long Tails

 A group of animals with long, striped tails appears high in the trees. One after another, the animals bounce along the branches. The animals are ring-tailed lemurs.

There are more than 70 different species (SPEE-sheez), or kinds, of lemurs. They all live on a huge island called Madagascar (MAD-uh-GAS-kar). Madagascar is near the coast of Africa. Lemurs belong to a big group of animals called primates (PRYE-mayts). Monkeys, apes, and people are primates too.

Many different kinds of lemurs live in Madagascar. This lemur is called a sifaka.

A ring-tailed lemur's tail is about 2 feet long. The tail is a bit longer than the lemur's body.

A ring-tailed lemur is about as big as a pet cat. It has a thin body and thin legs. Its tail is longer than its body.

A ring-tail's body is covered with soft, thick fur. The fur on the lemur's back is brownish gray.

Its belly has white fur. Its tail has rings of black-and-white fur.

A ring-tailed lemur's face and ears are white. Its eyes are yellow. Black fur surrounds the lemur's eyes and nose.

The ring-tailed lemur's scientific name is Lemur catta.

Most of a ring-tail's teeth point up or down, like your teeth do. But six teeth point straight forward. These teeth are called the toothcomb. A ring-tailed lemur uses its toothcomb to comb and clean its fur. Cleaning fur is called grooming.

This lemur is using its toothcomb to groom its tail.

Ring-tails are good jumpers. This one is jumping down from a tree.

Ring-tails spend a lot of time in trees. They use their hands and feet to climb. They leap from branch to branch. They can travel very quickly this way. But the lemurs also spend a lot of time on the ground. They walk on all four legs, like a cat.

Chapter 2

This ring-tailed lemur lives in a very dry forest. What is a ring-tail's neighborhood called?

The Ring-Tail's Home

The place where a kind of animal can live is called its habitat (HAB-uh-tat). Most ring-tailed lemurs live in forest habitats. Some of them live in thick forests full of tall trees. Others live in very dry forests. The trees in these forests look like spiny cactus plants.

Ring-tailed lemurs are social (SOH-shuhl) animals. Social animals live together in groups. A group of ring-tails is called a troop. There are as many as 25 lemurs in a troop. Each troop lives in its own neighborhood. This neighborhood is called a home range.

Ring-tails take a short rest during the hottest part of the day.

Ring-tailed lemurs mark the edges of their home range. Ring-tails' bodies make a smelly substance called scent (SENT). The lemurs rub scent on trees along the edges of their home range. These scent marks are messages for other troops of lemurs. The messages tell other lemurs to go away.

Ring-tails do handstands to rub their scent on trees.

These lemurs are looking for food.

Ring-tailed lemurs are diurnal (dye-UR-nuhl). Diurnal animals are most active during the day. Each troop of ring-tails spends most of the day traveling through its home range. The lemurs look for food and water as they go.

Sometimes ring-tails eat flowers.

Ring-tailed lemurs eat mostly fruit. They eat figs and the fruits of tamarind (TA-muh-rihnd) trees. They also eat leaves and other plant parts. Sometimes they eat insects and other small animals.

In the driest forests, water can be hard to find. Ring-tailed lemurs get water by eating juicy fruits and plants. They look for puddles of water in holes in trees. They also drink drops of dew (DOO).

Each evening, the whole troop travels together to two or three big trees. This is where the lemurs will rest for the night. The ring-tails climb high into the trees' branches. They stay in the trees until morning.

Ring-tailed lemurs sleep close together on tree branches.

Lemurs cuddle together to keep one another warm.

The ring-tailed lemur's habitat is often very warm during the day. But it can get cold at night. On cold nights, the ring-tails cuddle together to stay warm.

In the morning, the lemurs warm up in the sun. All the troop members sit together. They stretch out their arms and legs. They let sunlight shine on their bellies. Soon the ring-tails are warm. They are ready to start looking for breakfast.

These ring-tails are warming up in the sun.

Chapter 3

A baby ring-tail is riding on its mother's back. Who leads a troop of ring-tails?

Girls Rule!

 A female ring-tailed lemur leads each troop. This female decides where the troop will look for food. She also decides where the troop will rest.

The troop leader decides where the troop will go next.

Female ring-tails always have more power than male ring-tails. But some males in a troop are more important than other males. Male ring-tails figure out who is more powerful by having stink fights.

Sometimes ring-tails fight. But usually the members of a troop get along. These two lemurs are playing.

In a stink fight, two males rub smelly scent on their tails. Then they hold their tails high and shake them hard at each other. The stink fight ends when one of the males gives up. The winner of the stink fight walks with his head and tail held very high. The loser holds his head and tail lower.

Ring-tailed lemurs spend a lot of time grooming other members of their troop. One lemur uses its toothcomb or tongue to clean another lemur's fur. Sometimes several ring-tails groom one another at the same time.

One ring-tail is licking another lemur's face to clean it.

Ring-tailed lemurs send messages to other members of their troop. They also send messages to other troops. The lemurs use their senses of smell, hearing, and sight to understand these messages.

This lemur is watching other members of its troop.

Ring-tails use sounds to send some messages. The lemurs can make many different kinds of sounds. Each sound has a different meaning. Some are friendly sounds. Others mean that something dangerous is nearby.

Ring-tails meow and purr like cats. They grunt, bark, and make clicking sounds. They also howl loudly. People can hear a howling ring-tail from half a mile away!

Sometimes ring-tails howl to warn other troops to stay away.

Ring-tails use their tails to send messages too. As they travel through their home range, they hold their tails up high. The tails are like striped flags. Each lemur can see where the others are. That way, none of the ring-tails get lost.

As they walk, ring-tailed lemurs hold their tails high.

This lemur is sniffing a scent mark on a tree.

Ring-tails use their noses to find out about other lemurs. They sniff other members of their troop. They also sniff scent marks left by other lemurs. By sniffing a scent mark, a ring-tail can tell if the lemur that made the mark is part of its own troop.

Each troop wants to keep other lemurs out of its home range. The troop does not want to share its food. But sometimes other lemurs come too close to a troop's home range. Then the two troops fight. This is different from the males' stink fighting. In these fights, the females do all the fighting.

Female lemurs stare and make loud noises to make other lemurs go away.

If the other troop doesn't leave, the female lemurs fight.

First, the female lemurs stare at the other troop. If the other troop doesn't leave, the females leap toward the other troop. They make loud noises. They try to scare the other troop away. Sometimes they hit or bite the members of the other troop. Finally, one troop gives up and leaves.

Chapter 4

A baby lemur is drinking milk from its mother. How much does a newborn ring-tail weigh?

Baby Ring-Tails

Female ring-tailed lemurs usually have one baby at a time. But sometimes they have twins. A newborn ring-tail weighs 2 to 3 ounces. That is about as much as a large chicken egg weighs. The baby drinks milk from its mother. This is called nursing.

The mother ring-tail takes her baby with her wherever she goes. A newborn baby holds onto its mother's belly. When the baby is about two weeks old, it starts to ride on its mother's back.

This young baby is holding onto its mother's belly while she eats leaves.

A mother lemur watches as her baby climbs a branch.

When the baby is three or four weeks old, it climbs down from its mother's back. It takes its first steps. At first, it stays very close to its mother. But soon, the baby starts to explore.

All the troop's babies play together. They wrestle together on the ground. They also play tag in the branches of trees. They go back to their mothers to nurse and to sleep.

Baby ring-tails are playful.

When a baby ring-tail is about one month old, it starts to eat fruit and other solid food. But it still drinks milk too. When the ring-tail is five or six months old, it stops nursing.

This baby lemur is tasting the tamarind fruit that its mother is eating.

Ring-tailed lemurs can live to be more than 20 years old.

Ring-tailed lemurs are ready to start their own families when they are about three years old. The young females stay with their troop. But the young males leave. They go to live with a different troop.

Chapter 5

*Ring-tailed lemurs
are always watching
out for danger.*

Dangers

 Animals that hunt and eat other animals
are called predators (PREH-duh-turz). Ring-tailed
lemurs are always watching out for predators.
During the day, the lemurs look above them for

big birds like hawks and buzzards. They watch the ground for dogs and snakes.

At night, ring-tails climb high into their sleeping trees. Sleeping far above the ground helps to keep them safe from fossas. Fossas are catlike predators that hunt at night.

This bird is a harrier hawk. Harrier hawks are predators that hunt lemurs.

This predator is a fossa.

When a ring-tailed lemur sees a predator, the lemur warns the rest of the troop. It makes noises that tell the others where the predator is. These warnings help other members of the troop to stay safe.

If the predator is on the ground, the ring-tail makes clicking sounds. If the predator is flying overhead, the ring-tail makes a screaming sound. And if the predator is sitting in a tree, the ring-tail chirps and moans.

The lemur on the right is watching a predator. The lemur on the left is calling out to warn the rest of the troop.

This big patch of bare ground used to be covered with trees. People cut the trees down.

Ring-tailed lemurs' most dangerous enemy is humans. Some people hunt lemurs for food. And people are destroying ring-tailed lemurs' forest homes.

Ring-tailed lemurs need trees. The lemurs eat the leaves and fruits of trees. And they sleep in trees at night. But people have cut down many trees in the lemur's habitats. Some trees have been cut down to make room for farm fields. Other trees have been cut down for their wood. People in Madagascar use wood for cooking.

This man cuts down trees to sell the wood.

Some ring-tailed lemurs live in special parks. In these parks, lemurs are safe from hunters. And people are not allowed to cut down trees in these parks.

This ring-tailed lemur lives in Andringitra National Park. People are not allowed to hunt lemurs in the park.

This scientist is studying ring-tails to learn more about how they live.

But other ring-tails are not safe. They do not live in the parks. If people keep cutting down trees in these lemurs' habitats, the lemurs will lose their homes. Many of them may die.

Ring-tailed lemurs have lived in Madagascar for thousands of years. But they need help. If people protect the lemurs' habitats, ring-tails will be around for many more years.

ON SHARING A BOOK

When you share a book with a child, you show that reading is important. To get the most out of the experience, read in a comfortable, quiet place. Turn off the television and limit other distractions, such as telephone calls.

Be prepared to start slowly. Take turns reading parts of this book. Stop occasionally and discuss what you're reading. Talk about the photographs. If the child begins to lose interest, stop reading. When you pick up the book again, revisit the parts you have already read.

BE A VOCABULARY DETECTIVE

The word list on page 5 contains words that are important in understanding the topic of this book. Be word detectives and search for the words as you read the book together. Talk about what the words mean and how they are used in the sentence. Do any of these words have more than one meaning? You will find the words defined in a glossary on page 46.

WHAT ABOUT QUESTIONS?

Use questions to make sure the child understands the information in this book. Here are some suggestions:

> What did this paragraph tell us? What does this picture show? Do male or female ring-tails lead the troop? What do ring-tailed lemurs eat? What are stink fights? What animals hunt ring-tailed lemurs? What is your favorite part of the book? Why?

If the child has questions, don't hesitate to respond with questions of your own, such as What do *you* think? Why? What is it that you don't know? If the child can't remember certain facts, turn to the index.

INTRODUCING THE INDEX

The index helps readers find information without searching through the whole book. Turn to the index on page 48. Choose an entry such as *sleeping*, and ask the child to use the index to find out when and where ring-tails sleep. Repeat this exercise with as many entries as you like. Ask the child to point out the differences between an index and a glossary. (The index helps readers find information, while the glossary tells readers what words mean.)

RING-TAILED LEMURS

BOOKS

Oluonye, Mary N. *Madagascar*. Minneapolis: Carolrhoda Books, 2000. Learn about the animals, land, and culture of the island of Madagascar.

Powzyk, Joyce Ann. *In Search of Lemurs*. Washington, DC: National Geographic Society, 1998. This illustrated book is about one scientist's adventures while studying animals in Madagascar.

Swan, Erin Pembrey. *Primates: From Howler Monkeys to Humans*. New York: Franklin Watts, 1999. Find out about the world's many different kinds of primates.

WEBSITES
Madagascar
http://www.enchantedlearning.com/africa/madagascar/index
.shtml
Learn about the big island where ring-tailed lemurs live.

Primate Printouts
http://www.enchantedlearning.com/subjects/mammals/primate/
index.shtml
This Web page has links to information on many different kinds of primates, including ring-tailed lemurs.

Ring-Tailed Lemurs
http://kids.nationalgeographic.com/Animals/CreatureFeature/
Ring-tailed-lemur
See photos, watch videos, and read facts about ring-tailed lemurs.

GLOSSARY

dangerous: harmful or causing danger

dew (DOO): drops of water that form at night on plants and other objects near the ground

diurnal (dye-UR-nuhl): active during the day

grooming: cleaning the fur

habitat (HAB-uh-tat): a place where a kind of animal can live

home range: the area in which a group of ring-tailed lemurs lives

nursing: drinking mother's milk

predators (PREH-duh-turz): animals that hunt and eat other animals

primates (PRYE-mayts): a group of animals that includes humans, apes, monkeys, and lemurs

scent (SENT): a smelly substance ring-tailed lemurs' bodies make. The lemurs use scent to mark the edges of their home ranges.

social (SOH-shuhl): living together in groups

species (SPEE-sheez): a kind of animal

toothcomb: six teeth on a ring-tailed lemur's bottom jaw that point straight forward. A ring-tail uses its toothcomb to clean its fur.

troop: a group of ring-tailed lemurs that live together

INDEX

Pages listed in **bold** type refer to photographs.